DUMB AS I WANNA BE

DUMB AS I WANNA BE

101 Reasons to Hate Dennis Rodman

David Hanson

Illustrated by Christopher Erkmann

AVON BOOKS NEW YORK

AVON BOOKS

A division of
The Hearst Coroporation
1350 Avenue of the Americas
New York, New York 10019

Copyright © 1998 by David Hanson
Illustrations copyright © 1998 by Avon Books
Illustrations by Christopher Erkmann
Published by arrangement with the author
Visit our website at **http://www.AvonBooks.com**
Library of Congress Catalog Card Number: 97-94409
ISBN: 0-380-79695-3

First Avon Books Trade Printing: March 1998

AVON TRADEMARK REG. U.S.PAT. OFF. AND IN OTHER COUNTRIES, MARCA REGISTRADA, HECHO EN U.S.A.

Printed in the U.S.A.

OPM 10 9 8 7 6 5 4 3 2 1

This book is dedicated to basketball fans everywhere who believe the game of basketball didn't need to be augmented with oft dyed hair and overblown hype.

acknowledgments

This book is possible thanks to the efforts of Stephen S. Power at Avon Books.

Chris Erkmann's illustrations raise the following text to a new level.

Jamie Forbes, my agent, thanks for taking a chance on me.

Introduction

Basketball rose to glory on the backs of men whose games overshadowed their person. Mikan, Russell, Chamberlain, Robertson, Erving, Bird, Johnson and Jordan. Now a new visionary is set to lead basketball into the 21st century. He has brought to the game the hard cross-checks of hockey, the appeal of a crossover media star, and most of all, the glamour of cross-dressing.

Dennis Rodman has proved that if an athlete wears a dress, changes hair color on a regular basis and concentrates on just one part of the game, he can rise to the heights of money and fame. Style over substance.

He began his career as a likable, quiet forward with a talent to rebound that few his size ever display. Times have changed. That same shy guy was recently voted the most pretentious sports figure of 1996. And it's all true, trust me. I'm a Spurs fan.

I followed the Spurs before David Robinson arrived. I knew the struggles of a team who suffered through a rare disease striking down a star player, and an uncommon bone problem taking down another key member to the rebuilding effort. These things all faded in comparison to the greatest curse that can be foisted on a club: the reality of having Dennis Rodman on the roster.

The 1995-96 season saw Dennis take some time off for personal reasons, separate his shoulder in a motorcycle accident, and still find time at the end of the year for a complete mental breakdown that cost the Spurs a shot at the NBA finals.

The Spurs did the only thing they could: trade Dennis for the Bulls' Will Perdue. During Rodman's run in Chicago, he became the best third banana in basketball. Today that means huge endorsement dollars, an MTV show of his own, and a new hair color every week.

In 1997, Rodman went on a media blitz. He made Barbara Walters' ten most interesting people list; he shot a movie with Jean Claude Van Damme, and he became a professional wrestler. What follows next is a wake-up call for America. One last chance for you to get out and save yourself. Remember how foolish you looked for embracing bell-bottom jeans and wearing leisure suits? Dennis Rodman is the leisure suit of the '90s. The following 101 reasons explain why.

DUMB AS I WANNA BE

DUMB AS I

#1

Believes the road to enlightenment is paved with self-promotion.

WANNA BE

#2

Proves P.T. Barnum right every time he takes the court.

Whenever he plays, always makes sure he has no visible panty lines.

#4

Considered too unstable to be the absent father of Madonna's baby.

#5

Considered, by some, a better rebounder than Wilt Chamberlain—the man who grabbed more rebounds and more babes (after discounting inflation) and yet never felt the need to be the next Ru Paul.

WANNA BE

#6

Strip show every time
he's ejected from a game.

WANNA BE

Always makes the extra pass,
or else he'd have to shoot.

Green hair plays hell
with my TV's contrast.

WANNA BE

Took fluid, graceful sport and turned it into hockey.

DENNIS: THE TIME LINE

1986-1987 SEASON

- Drafted 27th overall by the Detroit Pistons.
- Averaged 4.3 rebounds a game and committed 166 personal fouls.
- Described as a "quiet young man."

WANNA BE

Least offensive and most offensive
player on the court at the same time.

DUMB AS I

#11

Designed the failed "halter-top" look
to replace current basketball jerseys.

WANNA BE

I got these from BONO!

"Thriller" Jacket

DUMB AS I

If the eyes are the window to the soul,
why does he always wear sunglasses?

#13

Hair dye causes environmental damage.

The picture of all those tattoos on sagging flesh when he's sixty.

WANNA BE

Ultimate team player, if the sport is golf.

Does all his scoring off the floor.

Auditioned for, but not cast in,
The Crying Game.

#18

Raises basketball offense to a new art form—minimalism.

Married himself. Granted divorce due
to irreconcilable differences.

DENNIS: THE TIME LINE

1987-1988 SEASON

- Gets taste of limelight by becoming a starter for the first time in his career.

- Averages 8.7 rebounds a game and commits a total of 273 personal fouls.

- Still described as a "quiet young man."

DUMB AS I

#20

On the court he's a player who does the little things: cheap shots, flagrant fouls, trash talking.

WANNA BE

#21

Fails in attempts to convince teammates that wearing Sheer Energy panty hose during games instead of socks would give them an extra burst of energy.

#22

As host of his own MTV show, he makes
Pauley Shore look like Dan Rather.

WANNA BE

Tattoos are really bizarre connect-the-dots puzzles that reveal the actual date of the end of the world.

Gratuitous tongue shot on
<u>Rolling Stone</u> cover.

DUMB AS I

#25

Wears hats that Huggy Bear
wouldn't be caught dead in.

WANNA BE

[#]**26**

Once wore white pumps after Labor Day.

When told team dress code included ties, arrives at airport with bondage equipment.

#28

Always gets rose facing wrong way
when he wears garters to play.

#29

The more media exposure he gets, the more physically exposed he wants to be.

WANNA BE

DENNIS: THE TIME LINE

1988-1989 SEASON

🏀 Debuts T-shirt reading "Have you hugged Bill Laimbeer today?"

🏀 Averages 9.4 rebounds a game and commits 292 personal fouls.

🏀 Still described as a "quiet young man."

DUMB AS I

Often called one of the warmest guys in the NBA, when compared with dry ice.

#31

Would wear mascara during games, but sweat always makes it run.

#32

Believes there is no team in "I."

WANNA BE

#33

Does have a sense of style
but refuses to use it.

With his role in the Van Damme movie Double Team has become part of the Six Degrees of Kevin Bacon game.

Sorry Kevin.

If he was on a sinking ship and cross-dressing, would he leave with the women and children first?

As a stunt to prove he was environmentally concerned, dons ill-fated chia-head look for a game.

Misunderstood coach who told him to develop some crossover moves.

#38

Believes phrase "Freedom's just another way of saying nothing left to lose" refers to clothing.

DUMB AS I

#39

Only NBA player with an endorsement deal from Victoria's Secret.

DENNIS: THE TIME LINE

1989-1990 SEASON

◎ Named Defensive Player of the Year.

◎ Averaged 9.9 rebounds a game and committed a total of 276 personal fouls.

◎ <u>Still</u> described as a "quiet young man."

DUMB AS I

Listens to Anthony Robbins tapes
backwards between games.

Claims everyone in the NBA gives cheap shots. He just gets caught because he's obvious about it.

#42

Those ears.

Would average twenty rebounds
a game if he wasn't so worried
about breaking a nail.

Slowed a step in recent years trying to cut down on runs in his stockings.

Should succeed at acting—
he's been doing it for years.

WANNA BE

Likes his salad like he likes his portraits—
no dressing.

Named his hands Monique and Judy.

You know why.

#48

For years the secret author of many of Barbara Cartland's novels.

DUMB AS I

#49

Tries purposefully to get body cavity
searched at airports.

WANNA BE

DENNIS: THE TIME LINE

1990-1991 SEASON

- Named Defensive Player of the Year, again.
- Averaged 12.5 rebounds a game.
- Averaged 3.4 personal fouls per game and 3.3 field goals made per game. In other words, he committed more fouls than he sank baskets. Remember, there's a limit of six fouls per game.

DUMB AS I

Guest starred as alien on
Third Rock from the Sun—not a stretch.

DUMB AS I

#51

Next movie role—<u>Bride of Frankenstein.</u>

Wanted to be called the next Deion Sanders when he heard the Dallas Cowboys star referred to as a two-way player.

Right in criticizing insane salaries
given to young, unproven talent.
Wrong in believing that money
should be given to him.

WANNA BE

#54

Wants to be remembered as best NBA player ever to act in a film.
Currently behind:

1. Jordan Space Jam
2. Kareem Airplane
3. Shaq Steel
4. Wilt Conan the Destroyer

DUMB AS I

Favorite car is convertible—that way
he can drive around topless.

#56

The thought of what his hair would look like if he grew it out.

After final game wants to show entire NBA arena his birthday suit. In the real world, they call that flashing.

DUMB AS I

When he ordered up an ego,
he paid the extra thirty-nine cents
to get it supersized.

Wears women's clothes,
but doesn't shave legs.

DENNIS: THE TIME LINE

1991-1992 SEASON

- Averaged 18.7 rebounds a game.
- Committed 248 personal fouls.
- The Detroit Pistons lose in the first round of the Eastern Conference Playoffs.

WANNA BE

Believes he should be treated differently off the court for what he does on the court, but not differently on the court for what he does off the court.

Spends a little more money on hair coloring, but he's worth it.

Forgot something blue for "wedding"
at Rockefeller Center.

Some players become larger
than the game—unfortunately,
he thinks he's one of them.

Personal motto–
"Show me the camera!"

Named the "Worst Dressed Woman for 1996" by the famed Mr. Blackwell.

WANNA BE

DUMB AS I

Has a bad case of Venus envy.

#67

By refusing to take shooting practice, he puts the thrill of uncertainty into layup attempts.

Considered Jackie Chan of the NBA—due to all the stunts he's pulled.

#69

Believes in physical play–sex
with Madonna, head butting refs,
and kicking cameramen in the groin.

DENNIS: THE TIME LINE

1992-1993 SEASON

- Made 183 field goals during the year. Committed 201 personal fouls.
- November 20, 1992–the Pistons suspend Rodman for three games for refusing to go on a road trip.
- March 1, 1993–Head butts Boston Celtics forward Xavier McDaniel during a game.
- No longer young, no longer quiet.

WANNA BE

To emulate Michael Jordan,
he will try out for the
Silver Bullets baseball team.

Makes a great team better,
a good team the same and
a bad team a carnival sideshow.

WANNA BE

#72

Has Bulls now considering new game night promotion: "The first one hundred to the stadium get to kick a cameraman in the groin."

#73

Won't discuss cup size, jock or bra.

Lobbying to be in remake of
Some Like It Hot.

If he were an accountant who one day decided to dye his hair, head butt an auditor and wear a Chanel suit to work, would he still have a job?

RODMOPOLITTAN

HOW MY
EGO
LOST
10Lbs!

BreAKiNG
THE
MYTH:
White pumps
after
LAbor DAy!

DUMB AS I

Could be first person to
get on covers of <u>GQ</u> and <u>Elle</u>.

Best pick-up line:
"I have that same dress at home,
wanna see it?"

Addicted to the warm, fuzzy feeling he gets from the cuticle remover fumes when he gets his nails done.

Sings duet with Crystal Waters on
Double Team soundtrack aptly titled
"Just A Freak."

DENNIS: THE TIME LINE

1993-1994 SEASON

- Traded to the San Antonio Spurs. Decides to start coloring his hair.

- Hits 156 field goals. Commits 229 personal fouls.

- December 18, 1994—Fined $7,500 for head butting Chicago Bulls forward Stacey King.

- January 4, 1994—Fined $10,000 for verbally abusing referees and refusing to leave the court during a game against the Los Angeles Lakers.

- March 3, 1994—fined $5,000 and suspended a game for head butting Utah Jazz guard John Stockton.

- May 2, 1994—fined $10,000 for kneeing Stockton and undercutting Jazz forward, Tom Chambers, during the same game.

WANNA BE

Was fined more last season than most people make in a year, yet believes the blue-collar worker understands him.

#81

Believes the way to beat The Man,
is to dress like The Woman.

#82

Mural of Dennis on Chicago freeway did not stop traffic because it chronicled the changing colors of Rodman's hair. Traffic stopped to see Dennis pictured in a suit.

Double Team co-star Mickey Rourke
thinks he's a good actor.

DUMB AS I

Now wants to do a Shakespearean play in the classical style, once he heard all the women's roles are played by men.

#85

First Album includes his own take on these timeless classics:

"I'm Every Woman"   "The Streak"

"Hit Me with Your Best Shot"   "Like a Virgin"

"I'm Too Sexy"   "Whip It"

"The Low Spark of High-Heeled Boys"   "I Feel Pretty"

and of course that international hit

"Dancing Queen"

DUMB AS I

Was upset after misunderstanding with shoe company over just what the "cross" in cross-trainer meant.

WANNA BE

Quote from <u>USA Today</u>, 2/10/97

"Rodman says he connects with the masses who enjoy watching a celebrity lead a high-profile lifestyle. He says it's like they are telling him, Reel us in black Jesus, black God. I say I'm going to be Moses. I'm going to part the Red Sea and (tell) everybody, 'Let's go. Let's have a good time over here on the other island.'"

Isn't this how Jonestown started?

Misunderstood premise for
Suddenly Susan TV show and
showed up to audition for the lead.

WANNA BE

Upset <u>Victor/Victoria</u> closed.
Wanted to play a man playing a woman
playing a man playing a woman.
Said he understood the part.

DENNIS: THE TIME LINE

1994-1995 SEASON

- Averages 3.2 personal fouls and 2.7 field goals per game.

- October 20, 1994—Spurs suspend Rodman for first three games of season because he throws a bag of ice at his coach, Bob Hill, and an official after being called for a second technical foul in an exhibition game.

- During season he will take a 14 game paid leave of absence and miss another 14 games due to a motorcycle accident that separates his shoulder.

- May 2, 1995—Takes off shoes and refuses to join team huddles after being substituted for late in the game.

WANNA BE

Believes all skirts should
be slit to the waist.

DUMB AS I

#91

Hasn't quite perfected sitting down
in a miniskirt and crossing legs
so that no one gets a peep show.

Hates people when they mob
him at Taco Bell, loves people
when they watch his MTV show.
Both are questions of taste.

Shoots free throws like he's
playing hot potato.

#94

Signs promo deal with Carl's Jr. after Wendy's refused to let him wear the red wig with ponytails for the commercial.

Keeps a lot of exotic birds
at home to chirp and drown
out the voices in his head.

#96

Fails as a photographer:
has a problem with overexposure.

Leads Detroit to how many
titles after Isaiah retired?

DUMB AS I

"They say Elvis is dead. He's not dead.
He's just a different color. He's 6' 8",
225 pounds, plays basketball,
and he's black."

—RODMAN QUOTED IN USA Today 2/10/97

WANNA BE

Acting has been compared
to the great Dolph Lundgren.

DENNIS: THE TIME LINE

1995-1996 SEASON

- ⚾ Traded to the Chicago Bulls.

- ⚾ January 12, 1996—In his first game as a Bull, fined $5,000 for verbally abusing referees and failing to leave the court after being ejected.

- ⚾ March 18, 1996—NBA suspends Rodman six games and fines him $20,000 for head butting referee Ted Bernhardt.

- ⚾ Tallies 146 field goals in the season and 196 personal fouls.

WANNA BE

Little known fact:
the sitcom <u>Bosom Buddies</u> had a
big impact on Dennis as a child.

Nicknamed "Worm," and much like the critter at the bottom of a tequila bottle, hard to swallow if you aren't completely smashed.

WANNA BE

DENNIS: THE TIME LINE

1996-1997 SEASON

- Rodman launches his own MTV show and shoots an action movie with Jean Claude Van Damme.

- December 10, 1996—NBA suspends him for two games for using obscene language on live TV following an ejection from a game with the Raptors.

- January 15, 1997—In Minnesota, Rodman falls into a group of photographers sitting courtside then kicks cameraman Eugene Amos in the groin. The NBA suspends Rodman for 11 games (the second longest suspension in league history) and fines him $25,000.

- Few people remember the days when he was known as a "quiet young man."